SALES TRAINING

POINTS & REMINDERS

for Automotive, RV & Boat Dealers

Mickey Moore

All rights reserved. No part of this book may be used or reproduced in any manner without written permission except in the case of brief quotations embodied in critical articles or reviews.

Copyright © 2019 Mickey Moore

ISBN: 978-1-7340966-0-6

INTRODUCTION

Top sales performers know that they cannot simply use their gift of gab to achieve great success. They know that success comes from applying the exact methods of the greatest salespeople in the world to their own way of selling. You will find that all top performers have their ears tuned into the voice of other top performers to learn something new that may help them reach their goals.

While top performers are constantly watching and listening for that something new, they are careful to filter out what does not line up with their goals. They only apply what will help them achieve what they need to do.

In other words, top performers know where they are going and what they need to do to get there. They study the greats to find out how they achieved their success without getting off track, off course. We all know those who rose to success quickly and fell just as fast, yet some stand the test of time. Those are the ones you want to model yourself after and mirror their every move.

Staying on course to reach your destination, is important, right? You bet it is! To reach any destination, you must first set the course you will take to get there and the slightest change in your plan, will take you off course. Those who fall fast are the ones who are not checking themselves along the way through life to see if they are still on course.

There is popular song that speaks to this. One lyric in that song says, "nothing crumbles in a day", it's a slow fade. To achieve success and keep it, we must watch our gauges, our compass so to speak. Pilots must do this in order to get to their destination, so we must.

You may remember in 1979, a DC-10 Passenger Jet flew from New Zealand to Antarctica on a sightseeing excursion on Air New Zealand flight 901. This 8-hour flight would provide passengers an experience of a lifetime: a chance to see the bottom of the world.

Unbeknownst to the flight crew, someone mistakenly changed the flight plan…typing a "6" into the flight computer instead of a "4" when entering the final number of the latitude and longitude coordinates.

This simple mistake changed the flight plan by a mere two degrees…a very small mistake…but one that changed the course of the flight eastwardly by 28 miles on the flight to Antarctica. This change took them from a sightseeing trip to a deadly one. This error put them on a collision course with Mt. Erebus.

This is what happens to many salespeople who rely on their gift of gab, instead of studying their trade or set their career course on the flight patterns of the greatest salespeople in the world. Many would call them "30-day wonders" because during their first 30 days they are selling on gab and enthusiasm, both of which are not reliable to achieve long term success.

The purpose of this book is to share what I know about the methods of the greats. This information will allow you to apply those methods to your way of selling. Methods to achieve similar or greater success.

The book is arranged by topics and their points to consider. This way you can quickly find the topic of your urgent need and study the points within to correct your course.

Good Selling
Mickey Moore

Topics

1. Get Ready for the Customer 1
2. Know Your Inventory Daily 2
3. Dealing with Helpers 3
4. Seven Things the Customers' Presence Tells Us 3
5. Meet the Customer 4
6. Investigation & Qualification Questions 5
7. How to Build Value 7
8. Financial Qualifiying Questions 8
9. Statements That Can Help You Close the Sale 9
10. Mental Ownership Must Occur
    Before Financial Ownership 10
11. Things to Keep in Mind as You
    Work with Your Customer 11
12. Eliminate Distractons 12
13. The Switchboard Operator 12
14. Selecting the Vehicle 13
15. Product Presentation 14
16. Product Demonstration 15
17. Park in the Sold Area 15
18. How to Handle "What's Your Best Price" 16
19. How to Handle "I Want to Think About It" 17
20. Walk Around Prospect's Trade 18
21. Service Walk 19
22. Purchase Refreshments As You Go to Your Office 19

23. Your Office and Evidence Manual 20

24. Prepare for Negotation 21

25. Secure Written Commitment to Own 21

26. Trade Appraisal 22

27. Get the Sales Manager's Proposal 22

28. Presenting the Proposal 23

29. Get the Manager Involved If Needed 23

30. What to Do If the Customer
    Will Not Agree to the Terms 24

31. Old School Card Box Customer Follow-Up System . . . 25

33. Prospecting 25

34. What the Pros Do 26

35. Social Media 27

36. Personal & Company CRM 27

37. Napoleon Hill's 17 Principles of Success 28

38. Recommended Reading 29

1. GET READY FOR THE CUSTOMER

1. The customer must like you!
2. The future of the dealership is in your hands
3. Someone will get sold
4. We sell feelings
5. First impressions are lasting impressions
6. Get ready to take control
7. Don't be afraid
8. You can eliminate all fear
9. Lead the customer, don't follow them
10. All prospects are of value
11. How do you look
12. How is your posture
13. How is your health
14. How is your attitude
15. The first sale is to sell yourself, the second is the customer
16. Are you sold on your product? Do you believe in your product?
17. Your passion for what you do will improve your voice tone and body language
18. Control must begin within seconds

2. KNOW YOUR INVENTORY DAILY

1. Review the new vehicle inventory-what was sold and what new came in
2. Review the used vehicle inventory over daily paying attention to fresh inventory
    a. Talk to the used vehicle manager about what they just purchased
    b. Let the used vehicle manager know what units your customers are looking for
    c. Talk to the salesperson who traded the vehicle for additional information
    d. Talk to the mechanics who serviced the vehicle

3. DEALING WITH HELPERS

1. Compliment the helper
2. Never argue or ignore them
3. Give them recognition

4. SEVEN THINGS THE CUSTOMERS' PRESENCE TELLS US

1. They have a want or need
2. They are considering your product
3. They are considering your dealership
4. The timing is right
5. They no longer want their vehicle
6. They want the price to be justified
7. They want to purchase from a professional salesperson

5. MEET THE CUSTOMER

1. Know that you cannot re-meet the customer
2. Meeting the customer begins when they know you are coming to them. At that point they will begin to form an opinion of you by what they can see. Your walk, speed, dress.
3. Smile and say: Welcome to Smith Motors. My name is _____ and yours?
4. Your first few words are more important than the rest
5. Words create feelings
6. People buy or do not buy based on feelings
7. The customer doesn't care how much you know until they know how much you care
8. You have a limited amount of time to take control of the customer
9. Make eye contact
10. Have a firm handshake
11. Write down the customer's name on your pocket notebook
12. Address the customer how they give you their name
13. Use their name during the sales process
14. Don't push it if they do not want to give their name to you at first
15. Always remember that you are a Persuasion Engineer. To find out what that means, read and study a book called "Persuasion Engineering" by Richard Bandler and John La Valle

6. INVESTIGATION & QUALIFICATION QUESTIONS

What you do **NOT** want to ask or say because it puts the customer in control

1. Can I help you
2. How are you doing
3. Would you like to drive this car
4. How much will you pay for this car
5. Why won't you buy
6. What is it you do not like about it
7. Why do you have to think about it
8. How much over invoice will you pay
9. What is the least you will take for your trade
10. What color do you want
11. How many months did you want to finance for
12. What is the most you can put down
13. Who else will have to help make the decision
14. Why do you like the other car better
15. Why won't you give any more
16. What other cars are you considering
17. Why do you feel your car is worth more
18. Can I be honest with you
19. Do you want me to tell the truth
20. Do you want my honest opinion

What you **DO** want to say because it puts you in control

1. Have you purchased here before
2. What influenced you to come to our dealership
3. Have you talked to anyone else here
4. Have you owned one of our products before
5. Do you live in the area
6. How long have you lived here
7. Where are you employed
8. Who will be the principal driver of this car
9. How many people are in your family
10. Will this car be used for family or business
11. How many miles a year do you drive
12. Was it new when you purchased it
13. How often do you normally trade
14. What other cars are you considering (only ask of they say they have been shopping)
15. What are you primarily looking for in your next car
16. What body style do you prefer
17. Do you like light, medium or dark colors
18. Is there any equipment that you prefer
19. What do you like about your current car
20. What would you like to have in your next car
21. Do you prefer fabric, vinyl or leather
22. Why are you looking for a new car today
23. How long would you anticipate owning it

7. HOW TO BUILD VALUE

1. Know your product
2. Know how to properly demonstrate the car
3. Find out what the customer's dominate buying motive is and sell the:
    a. Comfort
    b. Size
    c. Style
    d. Convenience
    e. Prestige
    f. Power, performance
    g. Economy
    h. Dependability
    i. Gas mileage
    j. Warranty
    k. Low maintenance
4. Properly show the features and benefits of the vehicle based on the customer desires
5. The MSRP is not an asking price, it is the market value
6. Avoid using words like thousands, hundreds, dollars, sticker price, we are asking
7. When you push up the perception of value, the perception of price goes down

8. FINANCIAL QUALIFYING QUESTIONS

1. Is this car titled in your name or your spouse
2. Where is the title
3. Is there a balance on your car
4. How did you determine the balance on your car
5. Does your pay-off include any insurance premiums or extended warranties
6. What type of budget are you considering
7. When is the next payment due on your car
8. What amount do you anticipate putting down
9. Who is your balance with
10. Do you have another car that you would consider selling or trading
11. Will there be anyone else involved in approving the decision

9. STATEMENTS THAT CAN HELP YOU CLOSE THE SALE

1. How may I be of service
2. Let me make you a proposal
3. If the figures are agreeable
4. Let's drive the car
5. If the monthly figures were agreeable
6. What do you like most about this car
7. Reward yourself
8. You deserve this car
9. If everything was right
10. Apparently, you have a reason for feeling that way
11. Other than price, what's most important to you
12. If we pay enough for your car would you own this car
13. If the difference was agreeable would you own this car
14. Let me share with you what we have
15. Do you prefer
16. Let's see what we have
17. Are you making all the buying decisions today
18. What do you like most about this car
19. Let's see about your taking delivery now
20. Congratulations
21. We will buy your car for its current market value

10. MENTAL OWNERSHIP MUST OCCUR BEFORE FINANCIAL OWNERSHIP

1. The customer must see themselves owning the car
2. Where will you be taking your first trip in you new car
3. Where do you park at your work
4. Will this car fit in your garage
5. Will this car be for a special occasion
6. What will you be able to do with this car that you cannot do with yours
7. Will these seats make your drive more comfortable
8. What kind of music do you play
9. Do you drive in the snow

11. THINGS TO KEEP IN MIND AS YOU WORK WITH YOUR CUSTOMER

1. A shopper is just shopping for the right salesperson
2. Turn the customer over if you are losing their attention or if there is just no rapport
3. A different personality can get a different decision
4. A salespersons dress, appearance, personality can influence feelings
5. When everything is right, but the customer wants to think about it, there is a problem
6. Do not prejudge or prequalify a customer
7. A salespersons job is to secure the commitment to own

12. ELIMINATE DISTRACTIONS

1. Never pick up the phone or cell phone when working with a customer

13. THE SWITCHBOARD OPERATOR

1. Do not underestimate their value
2. They talk to all your customers
3. They are your eyes and ears when you are not in the showroom
4. Treat them as though you cannot succeed without them

14. SELECTING THE VEHICLE

1. To a customer, your dealership may look like a sea of vehicles that they could get lost in.
2. So, do not just walk the customer around. This will only confuse them.
3. Take control by asking the customer what kind of vehicle they were looking for, then:
    a. If you **have what they want**, take them directly to that vehicle. Pull it out from its parking space and into the drive lane
    b. If you **do not have** what they want, then walk them to ones that are close to what they want
    Note: However, you must know your inventory in order to know your correct action
4. **"Never"** tell a prospect you don't have the car they want

15. PRODUCT PRESENTATION

1. Pull the vehicle out of the line and into the drive area
2. Open doors, hood, trunk and turn on the appropriate climate control
3. Perform a walk around presentation focusing on their dominant buying motives:
   a. Comfort
   b. Size
   c. Style
   d. Convenience
   e. Prestige
   f. Power, performance
   g. Economy
   h. Dependability
   i. Gas mileage
   j. Warranty
   k. Low maintenance

16. PRODUCT DEMONSTRATION

4. Salesperson always drives first
5. Have a pre-planned route, avoiding left hand turns
6. Review features, advantages and benefit as you drive
7. Halfway through the pre-planned route allow the customer to drive the car back
8. No more selling during the ride back. Only answer questions.

17. PARK IN THE SOLD AREA

1. As a trial close, direct the customer to park in the sold area
2. Say, if you think you may like to own this vehicle just park in over there in the sold area
    a. If the customer parks in the sold area, then assume the sale
    b. If the customer does not park in the sold area, then ask what additional features they would like
3. The customer should state their objection, then just switch them to the right car

18. HOW TO HANDLE "WHAT'S YOUR BEST PRICE"

1. By-pass the question
2. I am a good salesperson and believe that I can sell you a car, but I am not good enough to sell it just by quoting a price. I believe that you, like most people would want to know <u>all</u> of what you are getting for the price, right?
3. With your approval, could I spend just a few minutes sharing some of the other features and benefits of this vehicle and our dealership and then I will be glad to give you the best price.
4. I will be glad to get that for you, but first, other than price, what's important to you.
5. I will be glad to get that for you but first, let me ask you this. If the price was right, is this the car you want to own
6. I will be glad to get that for you and I want you to know that we have never lost a customer due to price.

19. HOW TO HANDLE "I WANT TO THINK ABOUT IT"

1. If everything was right, would you own this vehicle
2. Apparently, there's something that's not just right, do you mind if I ask what it is
3. Is it the color, trim
4. Is it the trade value
5. Is the new vehicle price
6. Is it the payment
7. Is it the product
8. Is it me

20. WALK AROUND PROSPECT'S TRADE

1. Let the customer sell you on their car so that you can sell the used car manager
2. Get excited
3. Ask about books and records
4. Ask about length of ownership
5. Ask about transferable warranty coverage
6. Ask about body damage
7. Touch but do not comment about dents, dings, scratches, interior tears, stains
8. Let the customers know that you have retail customers who would buy this car
9. Make sure that they know you want their car

21. SERVICE WALK

1. Introduce the customer to the service manager
2. Walk the customer around the shop
3. Share with them the benefits of a good service department

22. PURCHASE REFRESHMENTS AS YOU GO TO YOUR OFFICE

1. Upon entering the dealership showroom, purchase the customer a refreshment

23. YOUR OFFICE AND EVIDENCE MANUAL

Remember people buy people, they do not buy things

Welcome your customers into your office as if it were your home

Your evidence manual should be sitting on your desk. Once they are seated, encourage them to look it over.

You Evidence manual reveals who you are, so it should include the following:

1. Certificates, diplomas
2. Military
3. Awards
4. Hobbies
5. Pictures of your family
6. Pictures of your dog
7. A biography of yourself
8. Certificates of training, college
9. Sales achievements
10. Testimonial letters
11. Dealership awards
12. Dealership news articles
13. Dealership history
14. Product reports
15. Quotes

24. PREPARE FOR NEGOTIATION

1. Do we have the buyer and decision maker present?
2. Is the prospect sold on the car?
3. Is the prospect ready to buy?
4. Do you have good rapport with the prospect?

25. SECURE WRITTEN COMMITMENT TO OWN

1. Fill out the worksheet and write this out: <u>(customers name)</u> agrees to own and take delivery now of <u>(the vehicle)</u> when the figures are agreeable ✓<u>(customer approval signature)</u>

26. TRADE APPRAISAL

1. Complete all information on trade appraisal form
2. Tag the customers keys
3. Assure the customer that you will get top dollar for their trade and remind them that you may also have a buyer for their trade.
4. As you leave them to get the trade appraised, reassure them you will be working hard to make this deal happen.

27. GET THE SALES MANAGER'S PROPOSAL

1. Take the deal worksheet and trade appraisal to the sales manager
2. The sales manager will fill out the worksheet with the proposed figures
3. Leave the trade keys with the manager
4. Return to the customer to disclose the manager's proposal

28. PRESENTING THE PROPOSAL

1. Share the market value of the new vehicle
2. Share that we will pay _____ the current market value for their car
3. Share with them the normal customer investment
4. Share with them what the monthly investment will be
5. Divide the monthly investment by 30 for a daily cost. Write it in.
6. Ask for their approval
7. Show them where to approve
8. Lay the pen down and wait for the approval

29. GET THE MANAGER INVOLVED IF NEEDED

1. Turn all customers, who will not commit to purchase, over to the sales manager
2. A new personality could change the customers mind
3. The customer can save face from positions made, with the sales manager

30. WHAT TO DO IF THE CUSTOMER WILL NOT AGREE TO THE TERMS

1. Walk the customer to their car
2. Open their doors
3. Get in-between the door and the customer
4. Tell the customer that you feel bad that they are not getting the car they were so excited about just moments earlier.
5. Ask them if it was something you did to cause this.
6. Ask them if it is the car.
7. Ask if there is anything you can do right now to make things right
8. Let them know that they deserve the car and you want them to have it
9. If you cannot get them back into the dealership for further negotiation, find out when you can call them back.

31. OLD SCHOOL CARD BOX CUSTOMER FOLLOW-UP SYSTEM

1. Remove a 5x8 monthly index card from the card box file on your desk
2. Fill in all customer information on the card and place it in the front of the box
3. The card remains in the front of the box until the customer is contacted
4. Upon that time, place the card in a month that you want to follow back up with them
5. At the beginning of each month, remove all cards from the month you are in and move them to the front of the box
6. All cards that are in the front of the box are to be contacted then placed back in month that the customer agreed for you are to follow up with them

33. PROSPECTING

1. Strike gold by taking over the customers whose salesperson has left the dealership
2. Strike gold by looking at the vehicles in for service to find potential buyers
3. Strike gold by looking at the vehicles in the body shop

34. WHAT THE PROS DO

1. They have a written sales and commission goal
2. They have a written plan to achieve that
3. They use a daily planner
4. They have a follow up system that builds for the future
5. They have bird dogs that send them customers
6. They have a vehicle needed list
7. They know every vehicle on the lot
8. They are never the last person to talk to the customer unless the deal is closed
9. They know when to turn the deal over to management
10. They let the manager return trade keys
11. They never give a final price
12. They promote aftermarket products sold in the finance department
13. They know what they must do to win
14. They sharpen their skills daily by reading and studying the greats in their field

35. SOCIAL MEDIA

1. Important marketing tool for selling yourself to those you know
2. It's an online evidence manual
3. LinkedIn has many tools that will help you succeed

36. PERSONAL & COMPANY CRM

Every dealership has a CRM (Customer Relationship Management) system or they will soon be out of business and the same goes for you!

You will not last long in any business venture if you do not have ways to keep customers coming back to you. Repeat and referred customers are the long-term life blood of any business.

To keep customers coming back, you must let them know that you care about them. To achieve that, you must stay in touch with them every month or they will forget all about you when they need a second vehicle, or to refer you to their friends when they are looking for a car.

In other words, you must decide if you are in business for the short or long haul. Assuming you are in it for the long haul, you must plant the seeds now to receive future business. Remember this, everyone may not do business with you now but somewhere, sometime, they will with someone. Take actions now that will bring them back to you.

Your dealership has a CRM, but you need your own. Investing in your own personal one will pay for itself many times over.

37. NAPOLEON HILL'S 17 PRINCIPLES OF SUCCESS

1. Definiteness of Purpose
2. The Master Mind
3. Applied Faith
4. Going the Extra Mile
5. A Pleasing Personality
6. Personal Initiative
7. A Positive Mental Attitude
8. Enthusiasm
9. Self-Discipline
10. Accurate Thinking
11. Controlled Attention
12. Teamwork
13. Learning Form Defeat
14. Creative Vision
15. Maintaining Sound Physical and Mental Health
16. Budgeting Time and Money
17. Using Cosmic Habit Force

38. RECOMMENDED READING

Napoleon Hill	*Think and Grow Rich*
Richard Bandler	*Persuasion Engineering*
Tony Robbins	*Unlimited Power*
George Clauson	*The Richest Man in Babylon*
Bagley Reese	*Beyond Selling*
Og Mandino	*The Greatest Salesman in the World*
Og Mandino	*Mission Success*
God	*The Bible* - it teaches us how to live life well

www.ingramcontent.com/pod-product-compliance
Lightning Source LLC
Chambersburg PA
CBHW061518040426
42450CB00008B/1687